BONNIE A ROSS

Leaving Corporate America

My Top 10 Surprising Discoveries Shifting from Executive to Entrepreneur

First published by Bonnie A Ross Coaching LLC 2024

First edition

ISBN: 978-1-963895-00-1

This book was professionally typeset on Reedsy.
Find out more at reedsy.com

To Keith and Marian, you are still inspiring your daughter.

The only real valuable thing is intuition.

Albert Einstein

Contents

Introduction

I'd like to begin by sharing that this book isn't a step-by-step manual; rather, it reflects the discoveries from my own experiences. Dreaming at my desk, I often wondered about the possibility of stepping away from Corporate America—a world I had been a part of for more than three decades. Yet, I never reached out to someone who had bravely made that jump. Looking back, it felt too risky. I knew it wouldn't take much to take the leap, and I didn't want anyone to know how close I was to making such a giant change. This book serves as the dialogue I wish I could have had with someone who had navigated this path.

I Left in Phases

Reflecting on the grand adventure that's been my life lately, it's hilarious to realize my subconscious had been plotting my great escape long before I consciously caught up. You see, like countless others, the pandemic era was a real eye-opener for me. The whole not needing to commute thing? Absolute enlightenment. For me, it sparked this wild idea to leave California. Where to? No clue, but definitely not where I was.

Since my job had gone full remote, I figured, why not lean into it? I sold my house, ditched most of my stuff, crammed the remnants into storage (yep, even the car), and bought an RV. My dog Edison—my road-tripping sidekick—and I embarked on a 14-month, 14,000-mile odyssey. This epic saga started with a blog you're invited to check out. (www.agirlandherdog.life)

Me and Edison On the Road

Looking back, it was like my subconscious was on a quest to find the perfect spot for a fresh start, even before the rest of me knew what I was doing. The whole adventure was a journey of self-discovery, and I let my intuition set the course.

But this wasn't just a physical journey. Oh no, some serious mental and emotional gymnastics were also going on. While I was on the road, working from picnic tables, coffee shops, and hotel rooms, the workplace had morphed—new bosses, new vibes, new everything after a big acquisition. After spending 17 years of my life in this place, I hardly recognized it. Initially, I tried to adapt, but eventually, I realized I was drifting further and further from my true self. Lionel Richie sang it best, "Everybody wants me to be what they want me to be. I'm not happy when I try to fake it, no, ooh."

Despite the inner turmoil, I had a master plan: stick it out for another five years to hit my retirement goals. Talk about resistance—I couldn't fathom leaving my executive gig. I was all in, seeking some satisfaction focusing on the creativity and challenges of my role, even if it was not nourishing or joyful anymore. But hey, I had a plan and was convinced I could endure anything for a few more years to reach my financial nirvana.

Fast forward, and there I was, living the van life with Edison, traversing the country, and connecting with folks in the most random places during the century's worst pandemic. During these encounters, I began to pivot towards a life of simplicity, authenticity, and genuine human connection. I was having soulful conversations between loads at the laundromat, over morning coffee in diners, and around campfires with other travelers. These people were living great lives free from the bureaucracy and politics of big business. They were beautiful in a way that Los Angeles has lost touch with in the entertainment-centric industries. I was waking up to a new reality, and once that happens, there's no hitting the snooze button.

Then, 14 months later, Asheville, North Carolina, happened. Never in a million years did I see myself falling for a place so different from my past life. Yet here I was, drawn to this vibrant city of art, music, craft beer, and breathtaking nature. Like many who live here, I couldn't pinpoint what pulled me here, but something about Asheville's healing vibe, possibly the spirit of the Cherokee Nation and its creative souls, just felt right.

My First picture after leaving California

By December 2021, I'd settled into a mountain home surrounded by cows, donkeys, and the stunning Blue Ridge Mountains. Continuing my corporate role remotely, I believed that this change would make knocking out a few more years a breeze. How wrong I was. Once you awaken to a life that resonates with your soul, there's no turning back.

My New Neighborhood

When the Ice Cracked

I had this one-off ice-fishing adventure when I was a kid, thanks to an elderly neighbor who decided I'd make a good addition to his expedition with his grandson. Growing up a fan of all things outdoorsy, I was all in. Picture this: the middle of a frozen lake, stepping into a cozy shed, and watching this old-timer expertly carve a hole in the ice. What an afternoon! He was the only one who managed to catch anything, but wow, the stories he told were the real catch of the day. Mid-tale, he suddenly paused, ears perked up like a deer. When I curiously inquired, he delivered his wisdom with an impish smile: "If you hear the ice crack, run." Little did I know this would become my life's unofficial motto.

Fast forward to December 2022. There I was, glued to a Zoom call, watching snow fall through my office window, holding a cup of hot tea to warm my hands. This call felt more like a suspense thriller than a leadership meeting. Rumors of budget cuts and looming layoffs were swirling around, thanks to the pandemic's lingering shadow and a merry-go-round of leadership changes that would make your head spin. The constant reshuffles had us all questioning which way was up.

As the call droned on, outlining the hazy horizon, that's when I felt it—The Ice Cracked. It's hard to pin down the sensation, but something inside me dramatically shifted. My entire being was broadcasting an emergency exit signal: Time to bolt. My immediate thought was, "I can't do this anymore. I am done."

I'd love to tell you I sprang into action, plotting my grand escape with the precision of a heist movie. But reality had other plans. Instead of a slick exit, I crumbled, spiraling into a mess that led me to take a leave of absence. It turns out I needed to hit pause and step away completely to patch myself back up and devise a plan that didn't involve freezing in place.

So, that's exactly what I did.

The Exit

Here is another important piece of the story. For years, I was juggling life as an executive at a massive company by day and moonlighting as a life coach, helping clients navigate big life changes by night. Pretty ironic, right? This side hustle of mine turned out to be a powerful guide, teaching me a thing or two about dealing with upheaval and giving me a solid backup plan for my next career.

As my time off started to run out, I had to face the music and tell my boss I wasn't planning to stay. In my head, I imagined this big dramatic moment where they'd beg me to stay, sharing just how much they needed me. But when I finally broke the news, the conversation immediately shifted to calendaring details. I just had to pick a last day. After nearly 18 years, this was how my exit started. That hit me hard. Here I was, thinking I was a key player, and it turned out I was more of an extra in the grand scheme of things.

That was a real eye-opener. We often trick ourselves into thinking we're indispensable at work, but this experience reminded me that's not really how it goes. Companies keep on rolling no matter who comes and goes. It's not something to be bitter about; it's just how businesses survive and thrive.

Feeling even more confident about my decision, I knew I needed a proper send-off to close this chapter. Again, with 18 years invested, all the projects I invested in, all the careers I cheered on, I wasn't about to let my final act be a goodbye over a Zoom call. The company wasn't about to foot the bill for a farewell trip back to California, so I covered it myself, knowing full well my days banking my executive salary were ending. It was an investment in my emotional health, I needed closure.

I was hoping for a memorable goodbye, but it was pretty low-key. My retirement party? A get-together in a conference room with food from the cafeteria lined up on a counter along the wall. The tables are bare. We pushed the tables together so we could all see each other. Sure, folks were nice in the hallway, making promises to catch up before I left, but most of those plans never happened.

Sharing this story isn't about complaining, it is about perspective and self-empowerment. It's about showing how we can build up all these stories in our heads—reasons to stay put, even when we're ready to move on, and how letting go of those stories can actually feel pretty good. I mean *REALLY* good! In a way, realizing all this and deciding to leave was a bit sad, but more than that, it was liberating. It was proof that my intuition was right and that I was strong enough to take a new path.

The First Morning

Returning to my beautiful mountain home, I woke up the following day with Edison snuggled under my arm, listening to him softly snore. I looked out the window at the mountains, Spring made everything glow light green and yellow. I laid there feeling profound freedom, a feeling that I had never felt before in my life.

This first year was a journey of ups and downs and, at times difficult lessons, and every moment of it was amazing and joyful. That first morning, I woke with the Sun. They say that the early bird catches the worm; well, it is the early worm that gets caught. So, I continue to wake up with the Sun every morning.

When I reflect on that first year, there are 10 discoveries that I did not anticipate when I decided to leave. So if you are a corporate daydreamer wondering what it's like to leave and what surprises might be part of the journey, then this book is for you.

That Morning on My Deck

Discovery 1: The Need to Heal

The moment I bid adieu to my corporate scene, I harbored this notion that all my woes—exhaustion, being on constant defense, the mental gymnastics, the whole fog of competing agendas—would magically dissipate. After all, it was the corporate jungle causing all this turmoil, so stepping out of it should be the instant cure, right? Wrong. So very wrong.

That first week of post-corporate life, I was all gung-ho, ready to get my new venture off the ground. But the more I pushed, the more my body pushed back—with a vengeance. I'm not talking about needing to indulge in a leisurely nap. I'm talking about being slammed by an invisible force, knocking me out cold for hours. It wasn't just alarming; it felt like Gravity had a personal vendetta against me.

In search of answers, I turned to a therapist who dropped a truth bomb that changed everything. She explained I was essentially going through a breakup. Not just any breakup but the end of a long-term, toxic relationship. Mind. Blown.

So, I embraced the breakup recovery protocol: naps (lots of them), ice cream by the tub, aimless walks, binge-watching marathons, heart-to-hearts with friends, tackling jigsaw puzzles, floating in inner tubes down rivers, and did I mention naps? I dedicated a whole month to this self-care fiesta, a no-holds-barred approach to feeling good and ditching the guilt of "should be doing" something productive. This self-imposed therapy session turbocharged my recovery like nothing else.

Floating Down the River

Before this, the longest I'd ever taken off work was a measly three weeks, and that was a one-off in my four-decade career. Usually, I was a one-week vacation warrior, occasionally splurging on a long weekend. But this month? It was revolutionary.

Gradually, my zest for life and ambition crept back. Fast forward a year, and I'm still on the mend. (Seriously.) Sure, the corporate hangover occasionally throbs, but it's more of a mild annoyance than the soul-crushing weight it once was.

So, here's the kicker, the headline of my post-corporate life revelations: healing and self-care aren't just nice-to-haves; they're essential for anyone looking to gracefully exit the corporate stage and not crash land into their next chapter.

Discovery 2: Open Calendar

For years, my calendar was a testament to a bustling career. This frenetic pace wasn't unique to me; it was woven into the fabric of our workplace culture. We'd multitask through meetings, half-listening while chipping away at our ever-growing to-do lists, and then spend evenings catching up on the workday's overflow. A "light" week meant clocking in 60 hours; more often than not, the weeks stretched even longer. My mornings began with a ritual of declining meeting invites where I was double or triple-booked. Meetings I led naturally took precedence. The next criterion was based on the leadership hierarchy.

Imagine, after over 30 years of this relentless pace, opening your calendar to find it empty, save for a solitary reminder to take out the trash two days from now. Suddenly, the constant buzz of meetings and obligations had vanished, leaving a silence so profound it felt like it echoed.

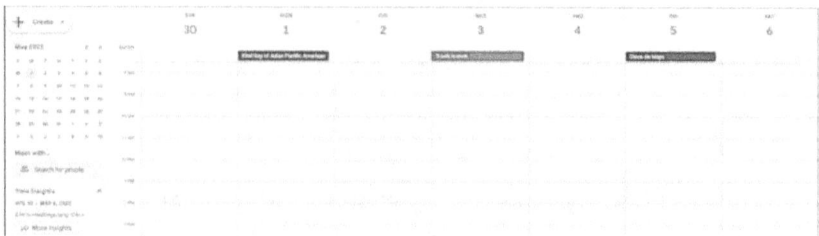

Oh, so empty

The absence wasn't just about the meetings. It was the loss of daily interactions, the sense of progress, and the strategic insights gained from those sessions. My calendar's blank pages symbolized a significant shift from a life of structured engagements to one of open-ended days.

I had always wondered about people who said they couldn't retire because they wouldn't know what to do with themselves. Standing at the threshold of this new chapter, their perspective suddenly made sense. The initial phase of adjustment was bewildering. It highlighted the importance of planning for such a transition and of finding new ways to stay engaged and connected.

I set a goal for myself: one meaningful engagement per day. I joined groups for entrepreneurs, remote workers, and those with a shared passion for coffee. I contacted former colleagues for monthly networking chats and signed up for various classes, webinars, and lectures. I met with neighbors for a fun evening together. This approach provided a semblance of structure, facilitated engagement, and helped me navigate the transition to a life that now depended on only self-motivation to progress.

The takeaway from this experience? It's crucial to balance meeting your need for community and avoiding the trap of over-commitment that defined so much of my previous life. We need engagement and connection to be balanced; for many of us, the workplace fills much of this need. The discovery of this immediate void was a big one for me.

Discovery 3: The Power of Titles

The first time someone hit me with the "What do you do?" question post-corporate life, I might as well have been asked to explain quantum physics on the spot. There I was, trying to articulate that I'm now an Identity Coach. And if that wasn't awkward enough, then came the follow-up—explaining what on earth that means, what my business is about, and how I guide people through transitions. To say it was awkward is an understatement; it was exposing and weird.

Having an executive title at a Fortune 100 company is like holding a magic wand (allusion intended). Doors fling open, people are happy to take your calls, and there's this genuine eagerness to partner. I remember the shift from manager to executive felt like being upgraded to first class on every flight. Suddenly, my ideas weren't just heard; they were amplified and set into motion. I used this newfound influence not just to elevate my projects but to boost others' ideas and careers as well. It was more than just perks and free parking; it was about wielding this power to fuel creative ventures and empowerment.

When I shifted to focus on my coaching business as my primary source of income, the transition was not about starting from zero but rather about adapting to an expanded context. I quickly realized that while I felt some changes at my core, the external perception of me had shifted significantly. No longer backed by the corporate identity, I found myself navigating the business landscape with different challenges. As a new entrepreneur, I was now viewed through the lens of the high-risk nature of startups, which starkly contrasted with the weight my identity once carried.

One aspect I cherished in my corporate role was forging solid, fun, and trust-filled partnerships. Those relationships were my sandbox, where we could play with ideas, weather storms, and celebrate wins. That sense of connection and mutual respect is what I've carried over into my new venture. Sure, my business card doesn't pack the same punch (yet), but leaning into authenticity has opened new doors in its own right. It's a slower ride but even more rewarding.

So, here I am, constantly recalibrating my self-image as I venture into uncharted territory. The discovery that the external perception of me shifted was more abrupt than a plot twist in a telenovela, but finding strength in my genuine self has been the real plot development. It's paved the way for new beginnings and given me the confidence to stride forward, even if I'm still figuring out the steps to this new dance.

Discovery 4: Financial Obligations

Embarking on the financial aspect of leaving corporate life was like deciding to hike up Everest wearing flip-flops—a steep learning curve with some painfully cold surprises. I thought I had it all figured out, with my spreadsheets detailing personal and business expenses for my fledgling Coaching venture. But then came the double whammy of taxes and healthcare, ready to crash my budget party.

During one of those pivotal chats with my financial advisor—right after we'd high-fived over my last tax filing as an executive—I casually asked what would change now that I was flying solo. She gave me this look, the kind that said, "Buckle up, kiddo," and simply stated, "Everything." Suddenly, I was diving into the thrilling world of quarterly taxes, paying into Social Security on my own, and keeping tabs on every expense. "How much should I squirrel away for taxes?" I naively asked. "Initially, about half," she replied without batting an eye. That first quarter, when I proudly made $2,500 and then waved goodbye to half of it, was my crash course in "Welcome to Entrepreneurship 101."

I quickly realized my income targets needed a serious upward revision unless I wanted to make ramen noodles a lifestyle choice.

And let's not even start on healthcare. The first time I saw the premiums as a newly minted entrepreneur, I experienced what can only be described as sticker shock on steroids. Thank the stars for the Affordable Care Act. That first year, my earnings from the corporate gig put me in a bracket that made "affordable" a relative term. Timing, as it turns out, is everything—not just in comedy but in healthcare enrollment, too.

This journey has taught me there's no such thing as a flawless exit strategy. Unanticipated expenses pop up with regularity. In my circle of corporate ex-pats, we swap tales of fiscal surprises like scouts trading badges. The cost of business insurance gobsmacked one friend; another wrestled with the labyrinthine rules of maintaining an LLC or S-Corp. The consensus? "There will always be something," a mantra for the financially initiated.

So, here I am, a little wiser, slightly poorer, and part of a community of corporate escapees, all learning to navigate the financial rapids of post-corporate life. It's an adventure, alright—one that often feels like you're assembling the plane on the way down. But hey, at least the view's incredible. The discovery here is there is no perfect plan, and no one has it completely figured out.

Discovery 5: Making Decisions

L et me share a little insight: the role of an executive isn't usually about making decisions from scratch. More often, it's about choosing the best option from a set presented by your team. Imagine being at a buffet where most dishes don't quite appeal to you, but your job is to select the one that best fits the occasion. Essentially, an executive's role is to keep the vision clear and guide the team toward making that vision a reality, even when the choices at hand seem less than ideal.

Embarking on my own venture was an eye-opener in many respects. I quickly realized that the luxury of having options presented to me was a thing of the past. Now, I was the researcher, the planner, and the decision-maker, all rolled into one. My natural curiosity and love for learning came in handy, though it also meant I had to develop a sharper focus to avoid getting lost in endless rabbit holes of information.

One of the things I missed initially was the dynamic exchange of ideas with colleagues from diverse backgrounds. Making decisions solo was daunting at first, but I gradually found my rhythm and developed a new approach to decision-making that was efficient and effective.

Take, for instance, the time I spent weeks perfecting a program, only to discover at the finish line that it didn't align with my overarching vision. There I was, laughing to myself at the realization of the stereotype of clueless management, and that clueless management was me. I needed to pivot, make new decisions, and not stay stuck. And so that is what I did, after a consolation pizza and beer with a friend.

Initially, every decision felt critical, as if a single misstep could derail my entire endeavor. However, I've since learned to view decisions as opportunities for growth and adaptation. The agility to swiftly correct course without the weight of corporate bureaucracy is incredibly liberating. In my solo journey, adjusting strategies or correcting decisions is a straightforward process, free from the ripples of emotional backlash and the resource-heavy toll it took in the corporate setting.

This journey has taught me the value of resilience, adaptability, and the power of a clear vision. I discovered the freedom and lightness of navigating my own path.

Discovery 6: Hearing "No"

J umping out of the corporate world into my own thing, I've bumped into some pretty funny realizations. But here's a kicker: in all those years in corporate land, I don't think I ever heard a straight-up "no." It's like we were all playing this giant game of verbal Twister, avoiding the word like it was cursed. If someone agreed, you'd get a solid "yes." But a "no"? That was a whole production, starting with a thoughtful "well..." followed by a saga of reasons that, had you known, you might not have asked in the first place.

Avoiding the word "no" is a powerful agreement in companies. Leaders are taught that that word stops problem-solving and creativity. It is a conversation stopper and idea killer. I still believe this is true. But step outside the office, and bam, the real world has zero issues with dropping a "no" bomb on you.

At first, hearing a straight "no" felt like I had been caught with my hand in the cookie jar. It immediately took me to my childhood again. It was abrupt like a door slamming shut. In the corporate bubble, "no" was the Voldemort of words—everyone knew it existed, but no one dared say it out loud. It took me a minute to get why I was taking "no" so personally. It turns out that I was reacting to the word itself, not what it actually meant. It was startling to me, like hearing a burp at the dinner table.

But here's what I figured out: outside the corporate echo chamber, "no" isn't about killing the conversation. It's more about signaling a mismatch, not the end of the road. Realizing this was like getting a new set of glasses—I could see things much clearer. I realized that "no" didn't have to be a full stop. It was just a signpost, saying maybe there's a better route to take.

And you know what? This whole adventure with the word "no" has been freeing. I discovered that in the bigger, messier, real world, "no" is just another word. It doesn't have the power to derail you unless you let it. It's actually kind of refreshing to step into a world where people say what they mean without all the tiptoeing. Now, when someone hits me with a "no," I just smile. It's a little reminder that I've left behind a world where you had to read between the lines to get the real message. And honestly, there's something pretty awesome about that.

Discovery 7: Routines

Routines, huh? Who knew they'd be such a revelation? Honestly, I never gave it much thought before, but it turns out that nearly everything in our lives orbits around our jobs. We wake up to alarms instead of sunlight, our mortgages stretch as long as a typical career span—about 30 years—and even our vacations are at the mercy of HR policies. But suddenly, without the anchor of a 9-to-5, I found myself floating in the open sea of an empty calendar. So, now what??

Over the years, I morphed from a night owl into an early bird out of necessity. My mornings started in the dark, squeezing in meditation and a walk before wrestling with rush hour. Breakfast? That was car cuisine. And if I was running late? Welcome to my mobile meeting room. I'd clock out at 5:00ish, battle traffic for two hours, and finally sit down for dinner around the time most folks are considering bedtime snacks. None of this was my idea of a good time.

For a while post-exit, I kept a version of this routine like a security blanket until it hit me: I had the freedom to design my day. What a novel concept! Turns out that our minds, bodies, and spirits are pretty opinionated about how we spend our time. Too much or too little of anything, and you're on a wild ride trying to find balance again.

This last year has been an eye-opener. I discovered that my brain hits its creative peak between 9:30 PM and 1:00 AM, making it prime time for creative work. Chores? Those are 10:00 AM to noon activities because, let's face it, you don't need a muse to do laundry. And meals? Those are now sit-down affairs at my table, not dashboard dining. The result? I've never felt more zen in my life.

Launching a business is no small feat; yes, it devours hours like nothing else. But here's the kicker: it makes all the difference when you work the right hours for you. I'm rolling with my body's rhythm now, working when I'm firing on all cylinders and resting when I'm not. And waking up with the sun? Game changer.

But let me tell you about the ultimate routine wrecker: the TV. When your days are packed and you're running on a tight schedule, TV is just another part of the evening unwind. But give a person too much free time, and suddenly, the TV morphs into this all-consuming vortex of distractions.

Navigating my newfound freedom meant reevaluating my relationship with binge-watching. Figuring out how to balance work, rest, and play without falling into the screen-time black hole has been an adventure. But hey, if that's the biggest challenge on this path, I'd say I'm doing alright.

In short, stepping away has been like taking the training wheels off my bike. Sure, there were a few wobbles (and maybe a crash or two into the TV-shaped hedge), but I've found a rhythm that works for me, not my Outlook calendar. The discovery in all this is that life's pretty sweet when you're not racing against the clock.

Discovery 8: Income

You're probably scratching your head, wondering why "income" is lounging at Discovery 8 instead of stealing the spotlight at Discovery 1. After all, isn't the terror of losing a steady paycheck and figuring out healthcare what keeps most folks glued to their office chairs? Well, income didn't end up being the boogeyman I expected. Sure, watching my savings shift downward little by little as I ventured into the unknown was a bit of a nail-biter. But then it hit me—if I'm not using this nest egg to chase a life where I don't hit snooze a dozen times every morning, what's the point of having it?

Diving from the steady cliff of regular paychecks into the wild rapids of entrepreneurship was definitely a "hold your nose and jump" moment. But, more importantly, it also made me face what I would become if I stayed put. Picture this: I have zero role models for gracefully gliding into golden years. My parents? They started their retirement countdown five years out, marking days off the calendar every day like prisoners waiting for parole. Burned out, exhausted, and just biding their time, they clung to the job for the paycheck. The kicker? Neither of them made it to the finish line; health took them out early. Now, if that's not a wake-up call, I don't know what is.

That moment when I felt the ice crack was the gut-punch realization that the so-called security of sticking it out was a mirage. I was pouring my heart and soul into a void, getting little joy in return. This epiphany was both devastating and, weirdly enough, probably what kept me from following in my folks' footsteps.

Facing life's hurdles, I've realized I'm at my best when I'm proactive, not just enduring the status quo. That's why income is bumped down to Discovery 8. I'm convinced that forging ahead with purpose is like sending out a bat signal for opportunities. Sure, it takes a blend of grit and a dash of daredevil, but as Panic! at the Disco sings, "Don't threaten me with a good time." So here I am, embracing the adventure, scrappy as ever, and ready for whatever comes next. So what was the discovery? I didn't have to repeat my parents' pattern; I could choose another path in their honor.

Discovery 9: Letting Go

Navigating the transition from leaving to truly letting go has been an insightful journey. Leaving, as straightforward as it seems, involves the physical act of moving on—you hand in your equipment, say your goodbyes, and physically depart from the office. Letting go, however, is a more nuanced process that unfolds over time.

Identity plays a significant role in this. Beyond just the professional title, it's about disentangling oneself from the daily drama and politics that once felt so integral. Despite stepping away, the curiosity about how things evolve without you can linger. It's a realization that the longer you stay emotionally invested in the old narrative, the more challenging it becomes to embrace your new path fully.

Another key insight I've encountered is the importance of not trying to influence an environment you've left behind. While offering guidance if former colleagues seek out your mentorship is rewarding, doing so without any residual bitterness is crucial. It's about providing support while also recognizing that your journey has taken a new direction.

For me, letting go has meant focusing on the present and the exciting possibilities that lie ahead. I've come to see my past experiences as a valuable collection of knowledge—there if I need it, but not something I actively contribute to anymore.

Admittedly, this process is easier said than done. The emotional ties to people and projects you've left behind can make the separation challenging. However, maintaining a connection that's too strong can hinder both your progress and your emotional well-being in the long run.

A significant turning point for me was adopting a daily ritual of setting intentions that align with my new goals. Each morning, I decide on three priorities: one aimed at growing my new business, another focused on building new social connections, and a third dedicated to personal well-being and connecting with nature. This practice has given me a clear sense of direction and a profound sense of purpose.

Gradually, my interests and energies have shifted towards activities and relationships that resonate with my current journey. My new focus is to engage with local entrepreneurs, form bonds with fellow business owners, and develop my business. As this shift occurred, the ongoing story lines from my previous role began to feel less relevant, marking a significant step in my process of letting go.

Discovering that moving on from the past isn't just about physical departure but also emotional detachment has been liberating. Letting go has become a healthy, healing process, allowing me to fully invest in the opportunities and challenges of my new life.

Discovery 10: Joy and Freedom

I f I were to rank my discoveries since making this leap into a new phase of life, joy and freedom would snag the top spot, no contest. It's like I've been handed the keys to a whole new world, where even the hiccups along the way come with a side of happiness.

I noticed it in others who took the plunge before me—they started to look like they'd discovered the fountain of youth, all bright-eyed and bushy-tailed. It turns out that that magic dust didn't pass me by; I've got people telling me I'm glowing. Apparently, this is what "healthy" looks like—news to me until I lived it. And it's not just me reaping the benefits; my dog is acting like a puppy again, and even my house plants are in on the act, greener and more vibrant than ever. There's a lightness at home that feels like someone turned up the brightness dial.

The folks I'm drawing into my life these days are a whole new crowd. Gone are the days of networking with people just because of the company name on my business card. Now, I'm vibing with creative souls focused on building something meaningful together. My venture into identity coaching is magnetizing clients navigating their own life changes. Witnessing their growth and creativity is always a jolt of inspiration.

Weekends used to be my recovery period—the time I needed to recuperate from a week's worth of job-induced turmoil. Now, every day feels balanced; I don't hit that Friday finish line feeling like I've been through the wringer. Sundays and Mondays are my official "chill" days, but they're about fun and rejuvenation, not just bandaging up the week's battle scars. It's about adding color and variety to my life, not just healing.

The confidence I feel in my decisions now is a game-changer. Looking back, I realize how much energy I wasted doubting my gut. There's something incredibly freeing about trusting your instincts. I used to feel like my head and heart were in a constant tug-of-war, but they're finally starting to play nice. I'm learning to let my heart lead the way more often, trusting it to come up with the answers my brain throws questions at. This might just be the natural order of things, and I'm all for it.

Joy was not a discovery per se; it is the richness and expansiveness of joy that was a great surprise.

Conclusion

s we reach the final pages of this journey, I want to clarify
an important point: this narrative isn't an indictment of the
corporate world, companies, or the traditional workplace setup.
I've gained a wealth of experience, knowledge, material gain, and, yes,
even joy from my years within those walls. The relationship between an
employee and a corporation is fundamentally about balance—a delicate
dance of give and take. It's akin to a well-choreographed ballet when
both parties are transparent about their expectations and contributions.
However, like any intricate dance, it's all too easy for the steps to get
muddled, leading one partner to feel overlooked or undervalued.

This imbalance, this sense of being on the losing end of the deal, is
where the harmony of the workplace can start to fray. Through sharing
my story, I hope to kindle a spark of reflection in you about your own
professional relationships. Is it symbiotic, nourishing both you and the
organization? Or has it tilted into a lopsided affair, leaving you drained
and disillusioned?

Navigating these waters requires a keen eye and a willingness to adjust
your sails when the winds change. If you discover that your current
course is more draining than fulfilling, I hope my experiences encourage
you not just to dream of different horizons but to pursue them. Fear,

that old familiar foe, has a knack for anchoring us in place, whispering doubts, and weaving tales of what-ifs.

Yet, here I stand (or, more accurately, sit with a pen in hand), having ventured into the unknown myself. It was a leap fueled by a desire for something more aligned with my heart's compass—a journey not without its storms but one that has led me to calmer, more authentic waters.

So, if you find yourself at a crossroads, feeling the tug of a heart-centric path yet hesitant to step off the well-trodden path, let my story serve as a gentle nudge. It's a reminder that while the leap may seem daunting, the other side holds the promise of growth, fulfillment, and, yes, a balance that resonates deeply with who you are and who you aspire to be. The journey to finding and maintaining that equilibrium, both within the corporate sphere and beyond, is a voyage worth embarking on. And who knows? The insights and transformations awaiting you might just make for an exhilarating chapter in your own life's narrative.

***

If you have enjoyed this read, please share your rating and insights by scanning the QR Code so others may also discover this book. Thank you!

More About Bonnie

Greetings! I'm Bonnie Ross, residing in the picturesque Buncombe County, North Carolina, alongside my loyal companion, Edison. Nestled in the enchanting Blueridge Mountains, we're surrounded by what I consider some of the world's most breathtaking nature. Throughout my life, nature has been my muse, mentor, and guiding force. Its intricate interdependence, perpetual renewal, and the transient nature of everything have left an indelible mark on me.

Drawing inspiration from nature's life cycles, I've woven resilience, intuition, strength, agility, and the power of patterns into the fabric of my life and professional practices. My journey is a mosaic of diverse experiences, global travels, encounters with brilliant minds, meaningful moments, and the resilience to overcome staggering tragedies—all of which shape my approach to coaching and mentorship.

In a mere five years, I ascended the corporate ladder from a coordinator at a statewide healthcare network to an HR Executive at The Walt Disney Company, triumphing over the aftermath of divorce and challenging jobs. Eight years later, I emerged not only debt-free but also well-invested. Certified as a coach in 2000, I initially focused on working with veterans and their families, later expanding to adults seeking purpose-centric life transitions. In 2023, as I concluded my 18-year career with Disney, I shifted my focus to individuals with untapped potential, blending my corporate executive experience with coaching and energy work.

My coaching style is vibrant and grounded in real-world insights, combining the energy of the Universe with the practicalities of corporate life. I believe in the power of intention and bring a 25-year corporate career to the table, aiming to support you holistically in your journey toward success and balance.

With over two decades of coaching and energy mentorship, I am a certified coach, energy mentor, neuro-linguistic practitioner, Reiki Master, meditation coach, Quantum Human Design specialist, Silva Intuition Method graduate, inclusion leadership coach, shiatsu bodyworker, and energy medicine professional practitioner.

In my professional background, I boast 25+ years as a corporate human resources professional, an 18-year executive tenure at The Walt Disney Company, certification as a Senior Human Resources Professional (SPHR), over two decades as a small business owner in coaching and energy mentorship, authorship, and public speaking engagements. My mission is to leverage this rich tapestry of experiences to guide you toward holistic success and balance.

Me and Edison in Nature

Resources

Lyrics | Lionel Richie | Easy. (n.d.-b). https://lyrics.lyricfind.com/lyrics/lionel-richie-easy

Panic! at the Disco – Don't Threaten Me with a Good Time. (n.d.). Genius. https://genius.com/Panic-at-the-disco-dont-threaten-me-with-a-good-time-lyrics

About the Author

Bonnie A. Ross is a multifaceted professional with over two decades of experience in coaching, energy mentorship, and holistic healing. With a foundation as a 20+ year Certified Coach and 25+ year Energy Mentor, Bonnie's expertise spans Neurolinguistic Programming, Reiki Mastery in Usui Shiki Ryoho, Meditation Coaching, and Quantum Human Design. Her qualifications also include being a Inclusion Leadership Coach, Shiatsu Body Worker, and an Energy Medicine Professional Practitioner.

Her corporate background enriches her practice, boasting over 25 years in human resources, including an 18-year executive role at The Walt Disney Company, and recognition as a Certified Senior Human Resources Professional (SPHR). As a 20+ year small business owner focused on coaching and energy mentorship, Bonnie has established herself as a published author and sought-after public speaker.

Residing in the serene Blueridge Mountains of Buncombe County, North Carolina, Bonnie draws profound inspiration from nature, integrating its lessons of resilience, intuition, and the power of patterns into her professional approach. Her diverse experiences, from global travels to overcoming personal tragedies, shape her holistic approach to mentorship and coaching, offering clients pathways to transformation and growth.

Bonnie's life and career are dedicated to fostering personal and professional development, utilizing an extensive toolkit of skills and knowledge to empower others towards achieving their fullest potential, all while maintaining a deep connection to the natural world that surrounds and inspires her daily work.

You can connect with me on:
🜨 https://www.presentlymecoaching.com
🖉 https://www.linkedin.com/in/bonnieross

Subscribe to my newsletter:
✉ https://www.presentlymecoaching.com/signup

www.ingramcontent.com/pod-product-compliance
Lightning Source LLC
Chambersburg PA
CBHW061326120626
46546CB00007B/2699